The Sinking of the Edmund Fitzgerald: The Loss of the Largest Ship on the Great Lakes

By Charles River Editors

The *Edmund Fitzgerald* in 1971

About Charles River Editors

Charles River Editors provides superior editing and original writing services across the digital publishing industry, with the expertise to create digital content for publishers across a vast range of subject matter. In addition to providing original digital content for third party publishers, we also republish civilization's greatest literary works, bringing them to new generations of readers via ebooks.

Sign up here to receive updates about free books as we publish them, and visit Our Kindle Author Page to browse today's free promotions and our most recently published Kindle titles.

Introduction

The Edmund Fitzgerald

"They might have split up or they might have capsized;

they may have broke deep and took water.

And all that remains is the faces and the names

of the wives and the sons and the daughters." – Gordon Lightfoot, "The Wreck of the Edmund Fitzgerald"

Sometimes there seems to be something almost mystical about a ship that is touted as the biggest or the best, almost as if fate cannot be tempted that much without striking a deadly blow. The Great Lakes have claimed countless thousands of vessels over the course of history, but its biggest and most famous victim was the SS *Edmund Fitzgerald*, the largest ship of its day to sail the Great Lakes and still the largest to lie below Lake Superior's murky depths.

The giant ore freighter was intentionally built "within a foot of the maximum length allowed for passage through the soon-to-be completed Saint Lawrence Seaway." but despite its commercial purpose, the *Edmund Fitzgerald* was also one of the most luxurious ships to ever set sail in the Great Lakes. One person who sailed aboard the ship recounted, "Stewards treated the guests to the entire VIP routine. The cuisine was reportedly excellent and snacks were always available in the lounge. A small but well stocked kitchenette provided the drinks. Once each trip, the captain held a candlelight dinner for the guests, complete with mess-jacketed stewards and special 'clamdigger' punch." Indeed, when it was completed in 1957, the *Edmund Fitzgerald* was nearly 730 feet long and dubbed "Queen of the Lakes", and it was so popular that people would wait along the shores to catch a glimpse of the famous boat.

The ship had already earned various safety awards and never suffered a serious problem when it set sail from Superior, Wisconsin with over 26,000 tons of freight on November 9, 1975 and headed for a steel mill near Detroit. During that afternoon, however, the National Weather Service, which had earlier predicted that a storm would miss Lake Superior, revised its estimates and issued gale warnings. Over the course of the next 24 hours, the *Fitzgerald* and other ships in Lake Superior tried to weather the storm, but by the early evening hours of November 10, the *Fitzgerald's* captain radioed other ships to report that the ship was having some problems and was taking on water.

In the ship's last radio contact, the captain reported that the ship and crew were "holding our own," but just what happened next still remains a mystery to this day. Minutes after that last contact, the *Edmund Fitzgerald* stopped replying on the radio and no longer showed up on radar, indicating that it sank, but no distress signal was ever given, suggesting something catastrophic happened almost instantly. At the time the ship went down with all 29 of its crew, winds had reached about 60 miles per hour, waves were about 25 feet high, and rogue waves were measured at 35 feet.

The wreck of the ship was found within days, and the fact that it was found in two large pieces suggest it broke apart on the surface of the lake, but it's still unclear how that happened. Since her loss with all hands, people from all walks of life have weighed in on the ship's fate, including official investigators, sailors, and meteorologists, but no one has yet to come to a clear conclusion about what exactly went wrong. Various theories have since been put forth, attributing the sinking to everything from rogue waves to the flooding of the cargo hold, but the loss made clear that more stringent regulations on shipping in the Great Lakes was necessary, and it was also a painful reminder of the dangers of maritime travel.

The Sinking of the Edmund Fitzgerald: The Loss of the Largest Ship on the Great Lakes chronicles the story of the Great Lakes' biggest victim. Along with pictures of important people, places, and events, you will learn about the sinking of the *Edmund Fitzgerald* like never before, in no time at all.

The Sinking of the Edmund Fitzgerald: The Loss of the Largest Ship on the Great Lakes

About Charles River Editors

Introduction

    Chapter 1: Designing the *Edmund Fitzgerald*

    Chapter 2: A Crew and Good Captain Well-Seasoned

    Chapter 3: A Hurricane West Wind

    Chapter 4: Water Comin' In

    Chapter 5: The Waves Turn the Minutes to Hours

    Chapter 6: Her Ice-Water Mansion

    Chapter 7: The Church Bell Chimed

    Bibliography

Chapter 1: Designing the *Edmund Fitzgerald*

The *Edmund Fitzgerald* in MacArthur Lock

"The lake, it is said, never gives up her dead

when the skies of November turn gloomy.

With a load of iron ore twenty-six thousand tons more

than the Edmund Fitzgerald weighed empty,

that good ship and true was a bone to be chewed

when the 'Gales of November' came early." – Gordon Lightfoot, "The Wreck of the Edmund Fitzgerald"

The ship later christened the *Edmund Fitzgerald* was the brainchild of the Northwestern Mutual Life Insurance Company, headquartered in Milwaukee, Wisconsin. Northwestern Mutual had been investing for some time in the mining and processing of iron and other similar minerals dug out of the ground around the Great Lakes, and in 1957, Northwestern Mutual became the first life insurance company in America to invest in a ship to haul the ore.

Since the company was already blazing a trail into new territory, its executives were determined to do it right. They contacted the Great Lakes Engineering Works (GLEW), located in River Rouge, Michigan, and contracted with them to design and build a ship that would be as close as possible to the maximum length of any vessel allowed through the almost completed Saint Lawrence Seaway. Upon completion, the ship was 730 feet long and 75 feet wide, with a draft of 25 feet. She was 39 feet tall from her keel to her funnel, with all but 6 feet of her depth utilized for holding cargo. As a result, the ship could carry approximately 26,000 long tons in her 729 foot hull.

A Coast Guard picture of the *Edmund Fitzgerald*

The long hull would later impress even experienced sailors who had sailed for years. Andrew Rajner, who served on the *Fitzgerald* for a few weeks in 1975, observed, "It's a funny feeling to walk down the ship and have that ship springing. Even if you go down the tunnel, it is a long way down to the other end. You have something moving underneath you, and you really are not sure of what you are standing on, but after a while, you get used to it. You just forget about it."

When the time came to name the ship, the board of directors of Northwestern decided to honor their president by naming their new investment the *Edmund Fitzgerald*. Fitzgerald's family was well-known in the Milwaukee area for civic contributions, but they also had a long nautical history. Fitzgerald's grandfather had been a captain on the Great Lakes at the turn of the 20th century, and his father owned the Milwaukee Drydock Company. Edmund Fitzgerald himself had spearheaded the idea of investing in a freighter, and his wife was chosen to swing the bottle of champagne that would christen the ship on June 7, 1958.

Fitzgerald and his namesake vessel

As with the launching of the *Titanic*, many of those who were among the 15,000 guests present that day would look back and wonder if the event itself had been some sort of bad omen, because when Elizabeth struck the bottle of the ship's bow, it refused to break. It took her two more swings to shatter the glass and spill the expensive liquid over the new hull. At that moment, the keel blocks were supposed to be snatched away and the ship was supposed to slide elegantly into the lake, but nothing happened. The crew scurried around trying one thing after another until finally, more than a half hour later, the ship was freed from its dry dock. Even then, instead of gliding into the lake, it lurched sideways and slammed into a nearby pier. More than three months would pass before the *Fitzgerald* finally completed her sea trials and was allowed to begin work.

Pictures of the launch of the *Edmund Fitzgerald*

For more than a decade, the *Fitzgerald* reigned supreme as the "Queen of the Lakes", with the *SS Murray Bay* her only rival in size. Not only was the ship large, the *Fitzgerald* was also safe; she featured a well-equipped pilot house with the best equipment available, and her three holds were divided by 21 steel watertight hatches. In 1969, the company installed a bow thruster that improved the ship's safety and maneuverability, and over the winter of 1971-72, she was modernized with oil burners to replace her coal-fired engines.

According to Delmore Webster, who had once served on the *Fitzgerald*, the ship was sturdily built and should have been able to stand some pretty bad weather: "When you are in a heavy sea, in heavy weather, it rolled. It wasn't in excess of other boats I have been on. I mean, it is not like she had an unusual characteristic for rolling." Another man, Richard Orgel, who also served on the ship concurred, saying, "When you are standing forward and looking aft it would remind you of a diving board just after somebody jumped off—the board, the diving board of a swimming pool. She did this whippingly…It seems that when the sea piles up under her stern and then falls away, she just doesn't drop down into the trough. The stern doesn't drop into the trough like you would expect it. It whips, is the best word—or springs, is the best way I could describe it."

That said, Orgel later recalled a conversation he had with Captain Ernest M. McSorley about a potential problem: "I asked him if it was possible that this action could actually cause the hatch clamps to come off. He said no, he had never seen that happen, and I remarked to him that there was sometimes a lot of action back there…He told me if she started working too much, I should alter course and call him. He said he was going to be laying on top of his bed. He wasn't going to undress or anything, and if I had any problems or thought it was working too much, I should call him." Given what happened in November 1975, it's possible that Oregel's concerns were eerily prophetic.

McSorley

Unlike many other freighters, the *Fitzgerald* was as comfortable as she was large. The J. L. Hudson Company designed her lavish interior and installed thick, plush carpeting and beautifully tiled bathrooms in the crew areas. The crew also enjoyed the comfort of air conditioning and meals prepared in a fully stocked pantry, and though the crew was relatively small, they dined comfortably in two separate dining rooms. The ship even included aesthetically pleasing features like drapes for the porthole windows and leather chairs in the lounge.

Anticipating that some of the investors might want to sail with the crew on occasion, the *Fitzgerald* was even outfitted with two comfortable state rooms set aside specifically for guests. Due to the comfortable accommodations available, guests were regularly welcomed aboard the ship, where they enjoyed amenities and dining similar to that found on small cruise ships. Playing to the crowd, the captain hosted at least one candlelight dinner for his guests each trip.

Following the *Fitzgerald's* launch, Northwestern leased her for the next 25 years to the Oglebay Norton Corporation, and she became the flagship of the company's Columbia Transportation fleet. During the 17 short years that she sailed, the *Fitzgerald* carried loads of taconite iron ore from where it was mined outside of Duluth, Minnesota and brought the loads to ports along the Great Lakes for processing. The *Fitzgerald* was a good and stout ship that had a reputation for being one of the best to ply the lakes, often setting new records for annual hauls and then turning around and beating those very records herself in the years that followed. Perhaps her most significant record was set in 1969, when the *Fitzgerald* hauled a load of 27,402 long tons, well over her designated limit.

Picture of the *Fitzgerald* unloading cargo in Toledo in 1960

On most days, it took about 4.5 hours to load the *Fitzgerald* in Duluth, two days to cross the lake, 14 hours to unload the freight at her destination, and two more days to make it back to Duluth. Thus, each round trip took about five days in normal seas, allowing the ship to make an average of 47 round trips each shipping season. By the time the *Fitzgerald* was lost, the ship had sailed more than a million miles.

As her reputation grew, so did her popularity among those involved with shipping. The *Fitzgerald* was the darling of many and given such affectionate nicknames as "Pride of the American Flag", "Toledo Express," "Mighty Fitz" and "Big Fitz", but her most prophetic and unfortunate in hindsight was "Titanic of the Great Lakes". Aware of the ship's reputation and popularity, Captain Peter Pulcer reveled in the *Fitzgerald*'s fame and regularly delighted ship watchers by playing music over the ship's loudspeakers anytime she was near land. When he was close enough to be heard by those on shore, he thought nothing about coming out on the deck and using a bull horn to entertain his audience with tales about the ship and her exploits.

The *Fitzgerald* was considered a good ship to work on and even won an award recognizing her excellent safety record in 1969. However, while the crew avoided injury, the ship itself did suffer a few minor mishaps, including running aground in 1969 and a small collision with the *SS Hochelaga* in 1970. The *Fitzgerald* also occasionally bumped the wall of lock when passing through and once lost her anchor. However, such incidents were common enough among such ships that these mishaps were considered part for the course.

Chapter 2: A Crew and Good Captain Well-Seasoned

"The ship was the pride of the American side coming back from some mill in Wisconsin.

As the big freighters go, it was bigger than most with a crew and good captain well-seasoned,

Concluding some terms with a couple of steel firms when they left fully loaded for Cleveland.

And later that night when the ship's bell rang, could it be the north wind they'd been feelin'?" – Gordon Lightfoot, "The Wreck of the Edmund Fitzgerald"

The day that the *Fitzgerald* began her fateful voyage, the ship was manned by an experienced crew whose members should have been prepared for anything that could happen. The captain, Ernest M. McSorley, was 63 and had been with the ship since 1972. In addition to that, he had been sailing on the Great Lakes for more than 40 years and had captained nine other ships before taking command of the *Fitzgerald*. His stepdaughter later told a reporter, "The sea was his life. He didn't even come home when he was sick. His whole life was built around the ship."

Among other crew members, McSorley was known for being a firm but quiet man, and he had a reputation for being a good man in a storm. One of the men who served with him said of McSorley, "He kept to himself much of the time. Your may see him in port when he goes down the ladder to make a phone call, but that's about all." Another observed, "He was a quiet guy on deck. He'd just answer your questions, but wasn't a guy who got into long conversations. In the pilothouse, with just the guys on watch, he had a great sense of humor and was very easy to get along with." A third man praised McSorley as "a very good man, competent, sober, about the best captain I ever knew." Whether it was fair or not, the fact that McSorley was in charge of all that took place aboard the ship also meant he would become the man who bore the brunt of the blame for the accident.

McSorley had been given the ability to select his crew, and he considered them professionals worthy of his respect and leadership, McSorley's First Mate was John McCarthy, a seasoned veteran from Ohio who was only one year younger than McSorley. The Second Mate, James A. Pratt, was 44 years old and also from Ohio, while the Third Mate, Michael Armagost, was a 37 year old from Iron River, Wisconsin. As the ranking officers on the ship, their decisions would later play into the events leading up to the wreck.

At 23, the oiler, Duluth native Thomas Bentsen, was among the youngest men in the crew, the other oilers were Blaine Wilhelm and Ralph Walton. Wilhelm was 52 years old when the ship sank and left behind a 12 year old daughter named Heidi, who would later remember little about his life: "I am not sure how he got into shipping, bur he was in the Navy before he began sailing on the Great Lakes. He had been sailing for as long as I can remember; I was only 12 when he died. On the *Fitzgerald*, he worked in the engine room." At 58, Walton was among the oldest and most seasoned of the men on board.

There were also three wheelsmen on board that night. John Poviatch was 59 years old and originally from far away Bradenton, Florida, while the other two were Eugene O'Brien and John Simmons. According to O'Brien's son, Eugene, "he began at age 16, and he was fifty when he died. He also worked in a glass factory for four years...so his sailing time was about 30 years...he would be gone from March-December and during that time he would only be home for about ten hours every five days. From January to March he was always home." On another occasion, he said in an interview that O'Brien's job "was to steer the boat basically, and navigate. He has a first mate up there and the captain usually isn't far behind." Simmons' granddaughter, Missy Clark-Nabozny, told a similar story about her grandfather: "He was on a ship prior to the *Edmund Fitzgerald* for six months and then spent his career on the *Edmund Fitzgerald*. He had been on the *Fitzgerald* since its maiden voyage. He started sailing when he was only seventeen years of age."

There were also three deck hands and one cadet, all in their early 20s. Deckhand Mark Thomas, 21, was from Richmond Heights, Ohio, and two other deckhands, Paul Rippa and Bruce

Hudson, were also from Ohio. California native David Weiss was the cadet and one of only three men on board who were born outside the Great Lakes region. He had only recently graduated from the Great Lakes Maritime Academy and been assigned to the *Fitzgerald*. The man who assigned him, John Tanner, believed that he was rewarding the young man for his hard work because the job on the *Edmund Fitzgerald* was considered a prize assignment. Instead, Tanner inadvertently sent Weiss to his death, and decades later, he wondered aloud, "I've watched his classmates. Thirty years later, they have families and children, in and out of college. What life would David have had? His classmates are captains and chief engineers. We take a lot for granted."

There were also three watchmen: William Spengler from Toledo, Ohio, Ransom Cundy from Superior, Wisconsin and Karl Peckol, from Ashtabula, Ohio. At 20, Peckol was the youngest man aboard. Cundy's daughter, Cheryl Rozman, later told the story of his life before the *Fitzgerald*: "He was born in Houghton, Michigan on April 16, 1922. After graduation from high school in Lake Linden, Michigan he joined the United States Marines. He fought in the Battle of Iwo Jima on February 19, 1945. After the war, he went back to his home in Lake Linden. My Grandfather introduced him to a captain of one of the freighters who serviced coal to the docks in Lake Linden-Hubbell ore docks. He was able to get my father a job on one of the boats. I think the first one was the Munch (National Steel Corp). Then he sailed on Albert Heekin & the Ernest T Weir. He sailed for National Steel Corp, Hanna Company & then for the Oglebay Norton Company. To my recollection he sailed on at least 5 or 6 of those company ships. Among them were the Reserve & the Armco. He had been sailing on the Reserve when he was one of the 'chosen' crew to go aboard the Str. *Edmund Fitzgerald* with Captain McSorley. He sailed on it for about 8 years. So he had sailed on & off for 30 years."

At 62, Robert Rafferty from Toledo was the ship's steward, while Allen Kalmon, from Washburn, Wisconsin, was the second cook. Frederick Beetcher of Superior and Nolan Church of Silver Bay, Minnesota, were porters, while George Holl of Cabot, Pennsylvania was the chief engineer. He headed a staff of four other men, all tasked with keeping the *Fitzgerald* in tip-top running shape: Edward Bindon, Thomas Edwards, and Russell Haskell all hailed from Ohio, while Oliver Champeau came from Sturgeon Bay, Wisconsin. Their work would be called into question when theories were put forth that the ship broke apart in the bad weather.

59 year old Joseph Mazes served as the ship's special maintenance man. He had no children of his own but was very devoted to his brother's kids, who called him Jugsy. According to one of his nieces, Carol Ross, "He sailed as soon as he got out of the service and he was going to retire very soon, and then the ship went down. He said to us a lot of times they didn't think they would make it with how rough the seas were. I remember a time he went to say goodbye to my dad, and went to his truck and then came back and grabbed his hands. It was like he knew he wasn't coming back, and he didn't."

The lowest ranking man on board was 30 year old Gordon F. MacLellan. Originally from Clearwater, Florida, he served as the ship's wiper. According to his niece, Sue Hill, he had returned to sail the Great Lakes as part of a family tradition: "My uncle had been on the *Fitzgerald* for about 5 years. My grandfather was a Master Captain who sailed the Great Lakes for about 30 years on a number of cargo vessels. My grandfather had even sailed the route that the *Fitzgerald* had taken a number of times. Needless to say, we all knew of the perils on the waters."

Chapter 3: A Hurricane West Wind

The *Edmund Fitzgerald* in 1971

"The wind in the wires made a tattle-tale sound and a wave broke over the railing.

And ev'ry man knew, as the captain did too 'twas the witch of November come stealin'.

The dawn came late and the breakfast had to wait when the Gales of November came slashin'.

When afternoon came it was freezin' rain in the face of a hurricane west wind." – Gordon Lightfoot, "The Wreck of the Edmund Fitzgerald"

Early in the morning on November 9, 1975, the *Edmund Fitzgerald* arrived at Dock 1 of the Burlington Northern Railroad in Duluth, and the weather was so cold that everyone was anxious to get the ship loaded and underway before the weather got any colder. Loading was not a problem as most of the men had been working together for years, and since it was nearly the end of the 1975 season, many were looking forward to getting the job done. Once winter truly came on, the *Fitzgerald* would not be able to sail anymore until spring, and some of the older men, like John Simmons, wondered if this would be their last season. Meanwhile, the younger men vacillated between speculating whether there was a better way to make a living and being thankful to even have jobs. The economy at that time was bad and getting worse, which meant there was also the constant threat that the factories themselves would be shut down. Manufacturing in America was becoming increasingly unpopular as environmentalist raised concerns about the impact of factories on nature, and some of those on board may have wondered about the unrest bubbling in the nation.

Of course, most of the crew was probably tired more than anything else. The load that day was 26,116 tons of taconite pellets, chunks of iron mixed with other ores that was mined nearby. The load was technically a little over the ship's official limit, but the Mighty Fitz had carried more and made it through just fine. The *Fitzgerald*'s job was to deliver the pellets safely to Zug Island across Lake Superior and up the Detroit River, where the pellets would be used to make steel.

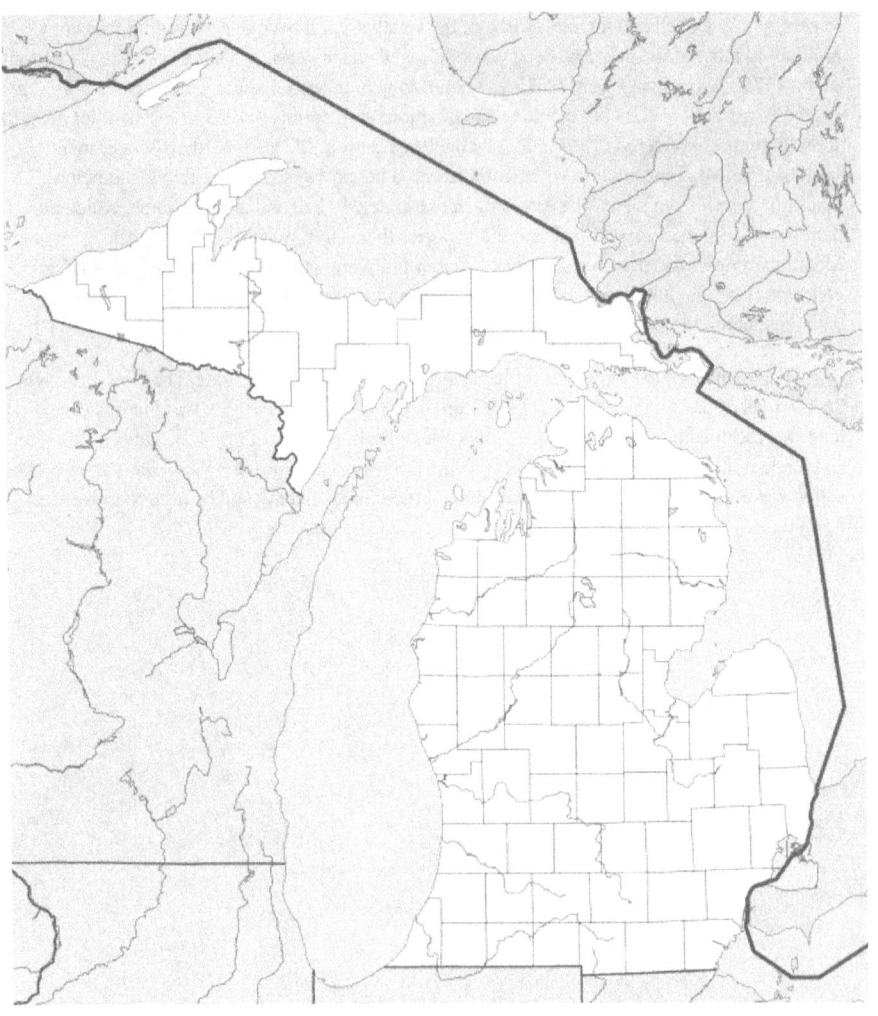

The route through Lake Superior to Zug Island in southeastern Michigan

The ship weighed anchor at 2:20 that afternoon, but less than 20 minutes after the *Fitzgerald* left, the National Weather Service issued a gale warning for the region. The storm was predicted to remain over land for the most part and pass south of the *Fitzgerald's* route, but Captain Jesse Cooper of the *Arthur M. Anderson*, another freighter making a similar trip that day, relayed the information about the weather to McSorley. At the time, neither captain was terribly concerned because gales on Lake Superior were common hazards in November, and both men and their ships had sailed safely through similar storms. Peter Pulcer, who had captained the *Fitzgerald* before McSorley, talked about the ship's handling of similar weather: "I have walked the walls already, I can tell you that. I have seen her roll too much. She would roll to a certain extent, but the seas on the quarter, they would come aboard and roll along the deck. I had never seen any damage done. She handled like a good little girl. That's all I know."

However, Captain Dudley Paquette of the SS *Wilfred Sykes* was not so sanguine about the forecast; his ship had left port just behind the *Fitzgerald* but decided to sail close to Lake Superior's north shore in order to avoid the brunt of the storm. He overheard the radio conversation between the *Anderson* and the *Fitzgerald* that led to their decision to take the usual route across the lake, but he refused to join them.

Sometime between 4:00-5:00 p.m. on the afternoon of November 9, the *Anderson* and the *Fitzgerald* sighted each other, but since the *Anderson* was bound for Gary, Indiana, the ships not remain in sight of each other for long. By this time, the *Fitzgerald* was running at full speed ahead, a little over 15 miles per hour, but around 7:00 p.m., the National Weather Service altered its forecast to include gale warnings for the entire lake. At that point, McSorley and Cooper agreed that they should both alter their courses and sail north toward the calmer waters near the coast of Canada, but this proved to be a mistake when the ships soon ran into another storm.

By 1:00 a.m. on November 10, the *Fitzgerald* was reporting that the wind was blowing at more than 50 miles per hour and 10 foot waves were crashing into the ship. Paquette, who was still monitoring the radio contact between the two other ships, was concerned to hear McSorley admit that he was slowing down the *Fitzgerald*'s speed due to the weather. By this time, the ship was about 20 miles south of Isle Royale, and according to records of the conversation, McSorley told Cooper, "We're going to try for some lee from Isle Royale. You're walking away from us anyway...I can't stay with you."

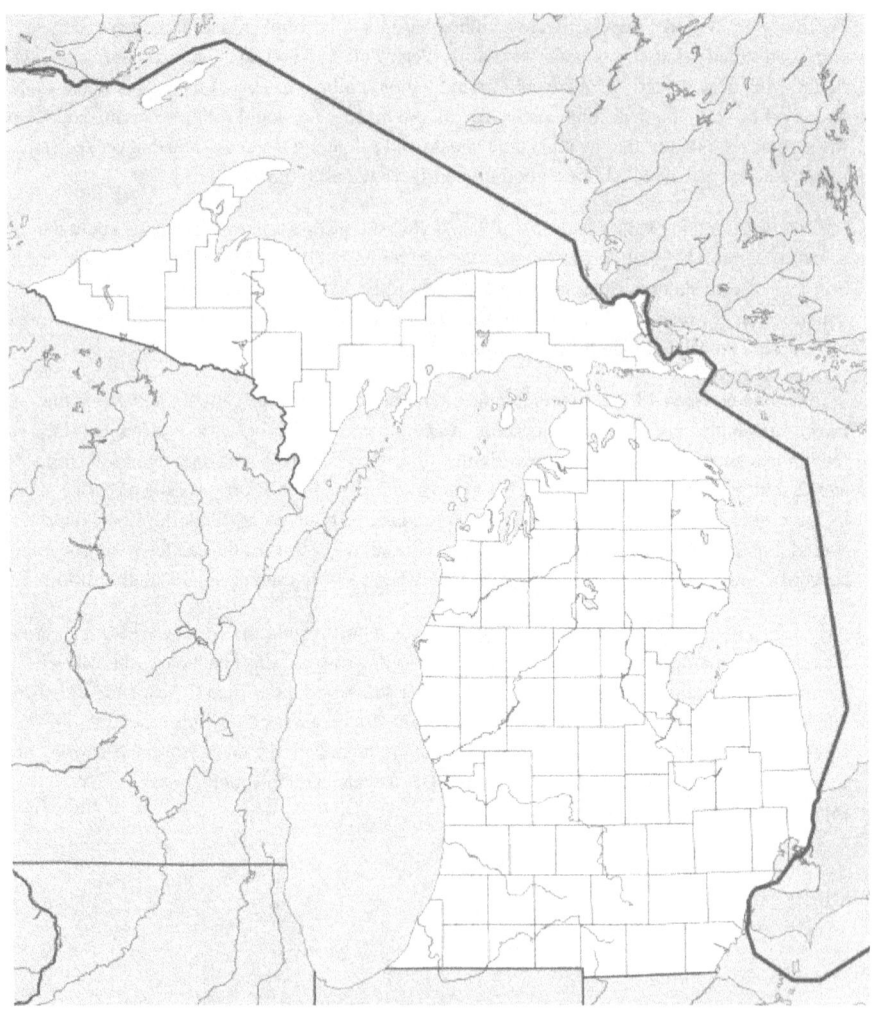

Isle Royale is one of the islands in the northwest corner of Lake Superior

At 2:00 a.m., the weather service reclassified the weather as a storm rather than a gale and sent out a warning that the winds could get higher than previously thought. The *Fitzgerald* kept the *Anderson* in sight over the next 12 hours as the weather became worse and worse, but by the early afternoon on November 10, McSorley decided to use the ship's larger engines to pull ahead of the *Anderson*, perhaps hoping to outrun the storm. At around 3:00 p.m., the eye of the storm passed over the two ships and shuffled the winds like a deck of cards. The winds constantly changed directions and also died down, but it also began to snow, making it more difficult for the men on board to see where they were going. It was around this time that the *Anderson* lost sight of the *Fitzgerald* for good.

Speculation still continues regarding the worst conditions produced by the storm, but in 2005, scientists at the National Oceanic and Atmospheric Administration (NOAA) teamed up with the National Weather Service to create a computer simulation of what the weather conditions were probably like that night. According to the simulation, by 4:00 on the afternoon of November 10, there were actually two storms hitting Lake Superior, and both had winds blowing in excess of 45 miles per hour. Unfortunately, the worst winds were in the southeastern section of the lake, where the *Fitzgerald* was sailing. Since the *Fitzgerald* was so heavily loaded, it was already sitting lower in the water than it normally would, which would have exacerbated the effect of the waves on the ship. Also, as the waves rolled over the top of the ship in one direction, they swirled around and pushed against the ship's deeply seated hull.

Chapter 4: Water Comin' In

"When suppertime came the old cook came on deck sayin' 'Fellas, it's too rough t'feed ya.'

At 7 p.m., it grew dark, it was then he said, 'Fellas, it's bin good t'know ya!'

The captain wired in he had water comin' in and the good ship and crew was in peril.

And later that night when 'is lights went outta sight came the wreck of the *Edmund Fitzgerald*."
– Gordon Lightfoot, "The Wreck of the Edmund Fitzgerald"

Watching the *Fitzgerald* from the deck of his own ship at about 3:15 p.m., Cooper noticed that the *Fitzgerald* was now rounding Caribou Island and commented to one of his crewmen that the ship was closer to the infamous Six Fathom Shoal than he would choose to be. 15 minutes later, McSorley contacted Cooper and alerted him that the *Fitzgerald* was beginning to take on water:

> McSorley: "*Anderson*, this is the *Fitzgerald*. I have sustained some topside damage. I have a fence rail laid down, two vents lost or damaged, and a list. I'm checking down. Will you stay by me 'til I get to Whitefish?"
>
> Cooper: "Charlie on that *Fitzgerald*. Do you have your pumps going?"
>
> McSorley: "Yes, both of them."

It was at this point, according to a report issued later by the National Transportation Safety Board. that water began to pour "into the ballast tanks and tunnel through topside damage and flooding into the cargo hold through non-weather tight hatch covers". This led the *Fitzgerald* to list to one side, even though the crew was running two of her six bilge pumps.

McSorley slowed the *Fitzgerald*'s speed, hoping that the *Anderson* would be able to get closer, and meanwhile, the United States Coast Guard sent out a warning letting all the ships in the area know that the Soo Locks had been closed because of the weather and that they should try to find a safe place to drop anchor and weather the storm. At around 4:10 p.m., the *Fitzgerald* radioed the *Anderson* again:

> *Fitzgerald*: "*Anderson*, this is the *Fitzgerald*. I have lost both radars. Can you provide me with radar plots till we reach Whitefish Bay?"

> *Anderson*: "Charlie on that, *Fitzgerald*. We'll keep you advised of position."

Now sailing blind, McSorley ordered the *Fitzgerald* slowed even more so that the ship could more easily share radar data with the *Anderson*, but McSorley could spot neither the lighthouse nor the navigational beacon for Whitefish Point. Unable to see it, he contacted the Coast Guard station in Grand Marais, Michigan on an emergency frequency and asked if they were working. It was then that he learned that neither the light nor the radio beacon was operational at that time, so McSorley began to radio other ships in the area to ask what they knew about the situation. Captain Cedric Woodard on the *Avafors* confirmed that both were indeed out. Later, the two captains spoke again:

> *Avafors*: "*Fitzgerald*, this is the *Avafors*. I have the Whitefish light now but still am receiving no beacon. Over."

> *Fitzgerald*: "I'm very glad to hear it."

> *Avafors*: "The wind is really howling down here. What are the conditions where you are?"

> *Fitzgerald*: (Indiscernible shouts heard by the *Avafors*.) "Don't let nobody on deck!"

> Avafors: "What's that, Fitzgerald? Unclear. Over."

> Fitzgerald: "I have a bad list, lost both radars. And am taking heavy seas over the deck. One of the worst seas I've ever been in."

> Avafors: "If I'm correct, you have two radars."

> Fitzgerald: "They're both gone."

By 7:00 p.m., the winds were blowing at almost 70 miles per hour, making the storm a hurricane, and a computer model later indicated that the worst winds and the highest waves (now up to 40 feet tall) were located at the very place where the *Fitzgerald* was fighting for her life. The *Anderson* was still nearby and also taking a beating, suffering damage to a lifeboat caused by a 35 foot wave. At 7:10 p.m., the ships contacted each other again:

> *Anderson*: "*Fitzgerald*, this is the *Anderson*. Have you checked down?"
>
> *Fitzgerald*: "Yes we have."
>
> *Anderson*: "*Fitzgerald*, we are about 10 miles behind you, and gaining about 1 1/2 miles per hour. Fitzgerald, there is a target 19 miles ahead of us. So the target would be 9 miles on ahead of you."
>
> *Fitzgerald*: "Well, am I going to clear?"
>
> *Anderson*: "Yes. He is going to pass to the west of you."
>
> *Fitzgerald*: "Well, fine."
>
> *Anderson*: "By the way, Fitzgerald, how are you making out with your problem?"
>
> *Fitzgerald*: "We are holding our own."
>
> *Anderson*: "Okay, fine. I'll be talking to you later."

As it turned out, the two ships would not speak later. By this time, the *Anderson* was fighting for survival against wind gusts up to 67 miles per hour and waves reaching 35 feet, the kind of conditions that explain how no one could see the *Fitzgerald* slip under the waves. In fact, it's possible the crew onboard the *Fitzgerald* didn't realize what was happening either, because no one issued a distress call or manned any of the lifeboats. The crash of the giant ship breaking apart and going down would have been drowned out by the wind and waves swirling around the *Fitzgerald* too. Regardless, when the crew of the *Anderson* looked at the radar just minutes after the last radio contact with the *Fitzgerald*, the ship no longer showed up. Thinking that perhaps the *Fitzgerald* was not appearing on radar because it had been screened by the storm, the *Anderson* tried repeatedly to contact the ship on the radio, but it was to no avail. The *Edmund Fitzgerald* had seemingly vanished without a trace.

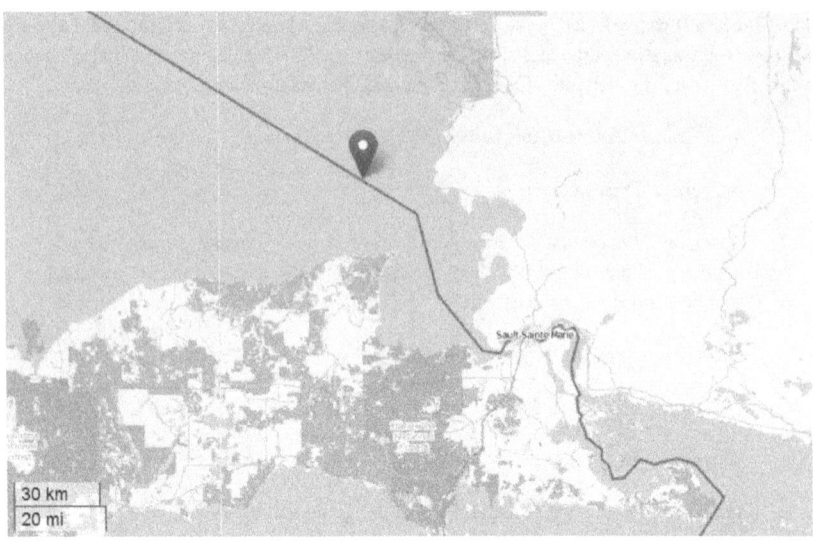

The final location of the *Edmund Fitzgerald* in Lake Superior

Nearly 40 years later, it still seems unlikely that anyone will ever know for sure what was happening aboard the *Fitzgerald* during those last desperate minutes, or what actually took the ship down. As Robert Manning, an expert on the event, put it:

> "A combination of problems culminated in her demise on November 10, 1975. She was probably overloaded. To be sure, she was loaded to her legal load limits for fall sailing, but those limits were increased a few years earlier and a change in her Plimsoll mark was authorized to allow but 11.5 ft. of freeboard compared to her original fall sailing requirement of 14.75 ft. The stresses on her hull and the weakening caused by those stresses over a period of time were overwhelming during the period of that November passage. The time was 1975...pre-global positioning satellite systems. Her method of navigation was radio direction finding, radar, and dead reckoning. With one of the critical RDF stations out of service at Whitefish Point, she was unable to get accurate radio cross bearings, both her radars were out and dead (from the abbreviation 'ded,' meaning deduced) reckoning is nearly impossible in a blinding gale, her position was often uncertain. She may have struck a reef between Caribou and Michipicoten Islands, she may have struck a shoal westerly of Caribou Island, we're uncertain if she struck anything at all."

Of course, the most difficult aspect of any accident of this nature is the loss of life. Manning himself admitted, "*EDMUND FITZGERALD* was lost suddenly. Not only was there no distress signal sent, and we do not know if the ship's general alarm was sounded, but even if it were, there would have been a very low likelihood of anyone surviving."

Chapter 5: The Waves Turn the Minutes to Hours

"Does anyone know where the love of God goes when the waves turn the minutes to hours?

The searchers all say they'd have made Whitefish Bay if they'd put fifteen more miles behind 'er." – Gordon Lightfoot, "The Wreck of the Edmund Fitzgerald"

At 7:25 p.m., the crew of *Anderson* radioed the Coast Guard to inform them of what was going on. The Coast Guard itself had suffered storm damage, including losing an antenna to the winds, but they called the *Anderson* back 20 minutes later to confirm that there was still no sign of the *Fitzgerald*. This time, the *Anderson* was instructed to call back on channel 12 in order to keep the emergency channel clear, and Cooper repeatedly tried to contact the Coast Guard again but could not get through again until 7:54. In the meantime, Cooper checked in with the *Nanfri*, another vessel on Lake Superior that night, to see if that ship had any contact with the *Fitzgerald*. After the *Nanfri* informed Cooper that the ship had no contact with the *Fitzgerald*, Cooper again contacted the Coast Guard at 8:32 and told them, "I am very concerned with the welfare of the Streamer *Edmund Fitzgerald*. He was right in front of us experiencing a little difficulty. He was taking on a small amount of water and none of the upbound ships have passed him. I can see no lights as before and don't have him on radar. I just hope he didn't take a nose dive."

A few minutes later, at 9:03, the ship was officially reported as missing, but according to Petty Officer Philip Branch, "I considered it serious, but at the time it was not urgent." The Coast Guard itself was overwhelmed by the storm and had no one to send to help, so they contacted the *Anderson* around the same time:

> Coast Guard: "*Anderson*, this is Group Soo. What is your present position?"
>
> *Anderson*: "We're down here, about two miles off Parisienne Island right now...the wind is northwest forty to forty-five miles here in the bay."
>
> Coast Guard: "Is it calming down at all, do you think?"
>
> *Anderson*: "In the bay it is, but I heard a couple of the salties talking up there, and they wish they hadn't gone out."

At the Coast Guard's request, the *Anderson* returned to the place where she had last seen the *Fitzgerald* and began a search for survivors, and by 10:30, the Coast Guard radioed all ships in the area and requested that they join in the search. The *William Clay Ford* and the *Hilda Marjanne* tried to help but were hampered in their movements by the storm that still raged, and it was nearly 11:00 by the time the first Coast Guard search and rescue aircraft arrived. Almost two more hours would pass before a Coast Guard helicopter finally arrived to assist with the search. Along with a plane from the Canadian Coast Guard, the aircraft searched the area for three days and patrolled the beach along the lake's eastern shore looking for survivors and wreckage. They found paddles, lifeboats and rafts, but no survivors or bodies.

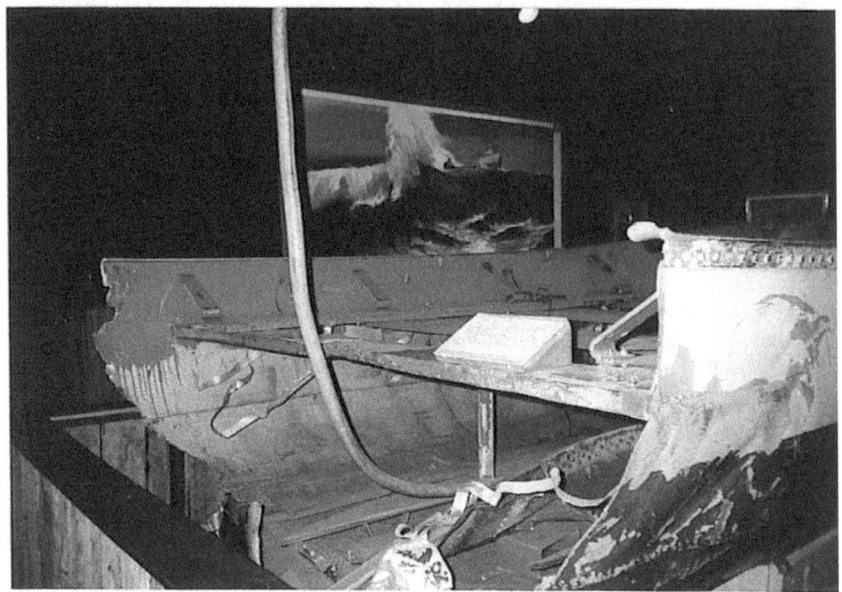

One of the *Fitzgerald's* wrecked lifeboats is now at the Valley Camp Museum Ship in Sault Ste. Marie Michigan.

Meanwhile, the families themselves started to learn about the *Fitzgerald*, and Cheryl Rozman, the daughter of crew member Ransom Cundy, was among the first to hear that something had gone terribly wrong: "We had heard on the TV on November 9th that there was a freighter missing on Lake Superior earlier that evening. Naturally my 1st thought was of my father. I settled to bed thinking & praying that he was safe wherever he was. The next morning I finished getting my 3 children off to school, the other two were not school age yet. I turned on the TV. There was a picture of the *Fitzgerald* & they were announcing it had sunk the night before with all hands missing. A search was going on to find any survivors. I had lost hope for my father's survival shortly after the *Fitzgerald* sank. Dad had told me earlier in my life that if this were to happen 'Cotton, I'd go down with the boat, because I can't even dog paddle.' I also knew that the temperature & waves on Lake Superior, no one could survive more than just a few minutes."

According to Carol Ross, the niece of maintenance man Joseph Mazes, "Oh, I was very very worried, and so scared that something was going to happen, and it did. I lived in Washburn (8 miles from Ashland, where Jugsy lives). I went to Ashland with my dad and sat by the phone calling the sheriff and anyone we could to try to get more information. Jugsy taught me to drive, and Margie too. We were so close to Jugsy."

John O'Brien was away from home when he heard about his father: "I found out about it because I was in college. In college, we didn't have cell phones like they do today. A police knocked on my door and told me I needed to call my mother. I was in Columbus, Ohio and she was in Toledo, Ohio. I went to a phone booth and she told me how the boat was missing and they didn't know much. Today we know everything instantaneously, but we didn't then. My initial reaction was to go back to Toledo. I wasn't aware of everything or how it happened. I thought initially they may have gotten in lifeboats, but a few days later no one was found in lifeboats, and my dad couldn't swim. So, I knew with thirty foot waves in the cold water of Lake Superior, none of them survived. It is wishful thinking - the people who said they were washed up on islands waiting to be found. In thirty-five degree water, with no lifeboat, in those kinds of winds and waves, they weren't going to make it. It only took a few days before we knew exactly what was going on."

It is shocking in the modern era, but many of the family members had to learn about the disaster from the nightly news. Heidi Brabon, the daughter of oiler Blaine Wilhelm, later recalled, "We found out through our neighbors who heard it on the 10 o'clock news. They came over to tell us they had heard mention of the Fitz, but due to a high school hockey game being televised we had to wait until the game was over to hear that channel's news broadcast. I remember being so scared and mom being on the phone most of the night trying to get somebody to tell her what was going on. I think we finally just sort of realized through the news broadcasts that he has not made it; it was on the national news. My sister was 9 months pregnant, and she had her child four days after my dad's death, but her husband had to keep the news from her until the baby's birth. I don't know how he did it."

Missy Clark-Nabozny joined her family in waiting for news of her grandfather, John Simmons: "We originally found out by phone call from someone who had been watching the news and my grandmother was at our house at the time. It was our whole family, my grandmother, and my mother and her sister. We got the phone call and then turned on the news and started hearing all the newsflashes coming out of Duluth. All we knew up until midnight was that it was missing, not that it sunk, but that it was missing. I remember it very vividly. We had to go to bed at 10:30 and we heard the adults in the living room talking, and later that night when they found out for sure they woke us up to tell us that it had sunk (the older grandkids) so that we knew what was going on."

In the end, there was nothing anyone could do. Clark-Nabozny added, "Well, like everyone else, it left us without any real answers. We had no place to go to pay our respects, and it left my grandmother a widow (she was a strong woman). Watching her struggle by herself was awful; you could see her sadness every time you brought it up. Mom was devastated along with her sister because she had nowhere to let it go, nowhere to say goodbye, and no way to deal with it. There were 9 of us grandchildren- the other eight might not have been impacted so much, but they saw our loss, and that hurt them."

Years later, many of those left behind by the men lost would work to come to terms with what happened. John O'Brien returned to college after his father's memorial service and explained, "I've been very blessed and I've got to give my dad a lot of credit for it. He was one to say, 'What do you want to be? Get an education. Don't be like me, working on a boat. Go to college, go to college.' It made me stay in college because college was a job. I was getting paid. Here was my dad, a guy with limited education, working on the lakes, yet he had the insight to do these things. A lot of people have great ideas, but they don't do anything about it. He was different. He went out and did it. He was very motivating for me. He got me moving."

Others chose to honor their loved ones by naming children after the relative or friend that had died, while some started scholarship funds for the families of needy sailors. Others worked and continue to work to understand what made the *Fitzgerald* sink in the first place, efforts that have led to stricter safety standards for all ships sailing on the Great Lakes. Though those 29 men lost their own lives that night, there is no way of knowing how many lives the tragedy might have otherwise saved, and while their graves remain little more than watery memories, their lives would continue to be celebrated for decades to come.

Chapter 6: Her Ice-Water Mansion

The anchor of the *Edmund Fitzgerald* on display at the Dossin Great Lakes Museum

"Lake Huron rolls, Superior sings in the rooms of her ice-water mansion.

Old Michigan steams like a young man's dreams; the islands and bays are for sportsmen.

And farther below Lake Ontario takes in what Lake Erie can send her,

And the iron boats go as the mariners all know with the Gales of November remembered." – Gordon Lightfoot, "The Wreck of the Edmund Fitzgerald"

While there was no real hope of finding survivors, the Coast Guard remained in the area for several days, using the same sort of radar normally used to spot submarines to try to locate the sunken *Fitzgerald*. Eventually, the Coast Guard found the ship at the bottom of Lake Superior on November 14, 1975, about 17 miles from Whitefish Bay, where the *Fitzgerald* might have been able to ride out the dreadful storm. The investigative team soon learned that the ship was broken apart into two pieces, leading many to speculate that the *Fitzgerald* had been split in two by the waves, but official investigations have concluded otherwise. Both the National Transportation

Safety Board and Coast Guard believe the *Fitzgerald* broke apart when the bow hit the bottom of the lake, and the Coast Guard's report stated, "The proximity of the bow and stern sections on the bottom of Lake Superior indicated that the vessel sank in one piece and broke apart either when it hit bottom or as it descended. Therefore, the Fitzgerald did not sustain a massive structural failure of the hull while on the surface...The final position of the wreckage indicated that if the Fitzgerald had capsized, it must have suffered a structural failure before hitting the lake bottom. The bow section would have had to right itself and the stern portion would have had to capsize before coming to rest on the bottom. It is, therefore, concluded that the Fitzgerald did not capsize on the surface."

According to Tanner, the man who assigned David Weiss to the *Fitzgerald*, "What we do know…is that she did take a nose dive to the bottom and in all likelihood broke in two when her stem (bow) struck the hard bottom while her unsupported after section was nearly vertical. In effect the 729' ship, going down in 530' of water, had 200' of stern in the air. That much ship, unsupported by water, would have caused her to breakup. Her breaking up is not what brought her down."

If the *Fitzgerald* didn't break apart on the surface, how did it sink? A couple of official reports have tried to answer that question. The Coast Guard report concluded, "The Commandant concurs with the Board that the most probable cause of the sinking was the loss of buoyancy resulting from massive flooding of the cargo hold. This flooding most likely took place through ineffective hatch closures. As the boarding seas rolled over the spar deck, the flooding was probably concentrated forward. The vessel dove into a wall of water and never recovered, with the breaking up of the ship occurring as it plunged or as the ship struck the bottom. The sinking was so rapid and unexpected that no one was able to successfully abandon ship."

If the ship sank because of a problem with the hatch covers, one question that is hard to face and difficult to answer is the extent to which human error played a part in the ship's loss. After all, if the ship didn't fasten enough hatches, it would allow the cargo hold to more easily flood. For his part, Paquette, the captain of the *Wilfred Sykes*, noted that McSorley "beat hell out of the *Fitzgerald* and very seldom ever hauled up for weather". He added that "in my opinion, all the subsequent events arose because (McSorley) kept pushing that ship and didn't have enough training in weather forecasting to use common sense and pick a route out of the worst of the wind and seas."

While there were many regulations and policies concerning how such a vessel should be maintained and prepared for a storm, there is also the reality that day-to-day work in any situation can often lead to a comfort level that copes with common problems so easily that a crisis can come as a shock. According to Manning, "Considering the weight of a cargo hatch, many crew in lakes' freighters were often nonchalant about the way the kestner clamps were secured. Not all of those clamps may have been battened down and considering the 'working' of the ship, her cargo hold may have been filling with water through the holidays in the cargo hatch and through the vent pipes carried away during the storm and maybe from a section of hull that was stove in while bottoming." That notion was echoed in a Coast Guard Marine Board report, which asserted, "The nature of Great Lakes shipping, with short voyages, much of the time in very protected waters, frequently with the same routine from trip to trip, leads to complacency and an overly optimistic attitude concerning the extreme weather conditions that can and do exist. The Marine Board feels that this attitude reflects itself at times in deferral of maintenance and repairs, in failure to prepare properly for heavy weather, and in the conviction that since refuges are near, safety is possible by 'running for it.' While it is true that sailing conditions are good during the summer season, changes can occur abruptly, with severe storms and extreme weather and sea conditions arising rapidly. This tragic accident points out the need for all persons involved in Great Lakes shipping to foster increased awareness of the hazards which exist."

In May 1976, the United States navy sent the unmanned submarine *CURV-III* to the wreck, and according to the information the unit sent back, the *Fitzgerald*'s bow settled on the lakes bottom in much the same way that it had once rode the surface. However, the stern lay upside down, and the midsection of the ship was in pieces and mostly obscured by piles of taconite. The Coast Guard report stated, "An area of distorted metal lies between the two pieces and to both sides over a distance of some 200 feet. Both the bow and the stern sections and all of the wreckage appear to be settled into the bottom mud, and a great deal of mud covers the portion of the Spar deck attached to the bow section. The bottom mud in the area of the wreckage shows extensive disruption and, in some locations, the bottom mud is in large mounds. The mud appears to be plowed up both at the bow and the stern sections."

The NTSB used the findings from the CURV-III expedition to assert that the ship flooded as a result of inefficient hatch covers. The NTSB observed, "The No. 1 hatch cover was entirely inside the No. 1 hatch and showed indications of buckling from external loading. Sections of the coaming in way of the No. 1 hatch were fractured and buckled inward. The No. 2 hatch cover was missing and the coaming on the No. 2 hatch was fractured and buckled. Hatches Nos. 3 and 4 were covered with mud; one corner of hatch cover No. 3 could be seen in place. Hatch cover No. 5 was missing. A series of 16 consecutive hatch cover clamps were observed on the No. 5 hatch coaming. Of this series, the first and eighth were distorted or broken. All of the 14 other clamps were undamaged and in the open position. The No. 6 hatch was open and a hatch cover was standing on end vertically in the hatch. The hatch covers were missing from hatches Nos. 7 and 8 and both coamings were fractured and severely distorted. The bow section abruptly ended just aft of hatch No. 8 and the deck plating was ripped up from the separation to the forward end of hatch No. 7." The Coast Guard believed that the hatch covers that were in perfect condition remained that way because they weren't actually fastened, and that water thus flooded into the cargo hold until the ship could no longer float. The NTSB blamed the sinking on "the collapse of one or more of the hatch covers under the weight of giant boarding seas."

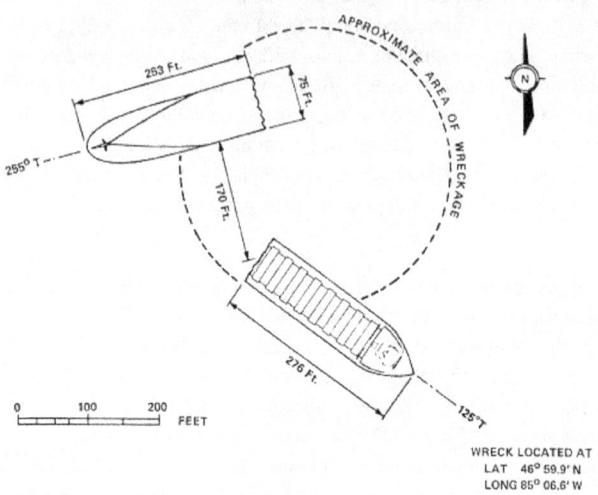

Figure 3. Sketch of relative positions of bow and stern section.

A Coast Guard model of the two pieces of the ship on the bottom of the lake

The *Fitzgerald* lay in that spot undisturbed until 1980, when Jean-Michel Cousteau, son of the famous underwater explorer Jacques Cousteau, sent two of his crew down in a manned submersible to examine the debris. Since the primary purpose of this dive was simply to gather material for a documentary about the Saint Lawrence River, little was accomplished that affected the understanding of the wreck. Then, in 1989, the Michigan Sea Grant Program sent a team to the wreckage to record video of it. The expedition included members of NOAA, the National Geographic Society, the Great Lakes Shipwreck Historical Society, the United States Army Corps of Engineers and the United States Fish and Wildlife Service. That expedition used the new Remote Operated Vehicle, known as the ROV, to explore the site.

These dives were designed and marketed as attempts to expand mankind's knowledge of the world in the submerged frontier, but the big question on everyone's mind was always about how the *Edmund Fitzgerald* actually sank. Again and again, different theories emerged, often with the next one contradicting the previous idea. For example, the dive associated with the Michigan

Sea Grant Program noted that the glass on much of the ship remained unbroken and that much of the other damage to the ship had been caused by more than just a storm. Like the conclusions of the NTSB and Coast Guard, this raised the question of whether there was some sort of weakness in the structure of the vessel itself. Author Frederick Stonehouse noted, "The Great Lakes ore carrier is the most commercially efficient vessel in the shipping trade today. But it's nothing but a motorized barge! It's the unsafest commercial vessel afloat. It has virtually no watertight integrity. Theoretically, a one-inch puncture in the cargo hold will sink it...Contrast this with the story of the SS *Maumee*, an oceangoing tanker that struck an iceberg near the South Pole recently. The collision tore a hole in the ship's bow large enough to drive a truck through, but the Maumee was able to travel halfway around the world to a repair yard, without difficulty, because she was fitted with watertight bulkheads."

In July 1994, Fred Shannon executed a number of dives and determined that the location in which the wreckage was located had shifted back and forth on several occasions since the *Fitzgerald* went down. Before he left the wreck following his seventh dive, Shannon left a memorial plaque on the ship's pilot house, and he concluded that "at least one-third of the two acres of immediate wreckage containing the two major portions of the vessel is in U.S. waters because of an error in the position of the U.S.–Canada boundary line shown on official lake charts." Following his dives, Shannon announced triumphantly, "All former theories are shot. They can go back in the closet. The extreme tearing pattern reveals evidence that the separation was not instantaneous. There are deep dents and buckles in the hull, but they don't indicate the boat struck a shoal." More notably, Shannon argued that the NTSB and Coast Guard were wrong to conclude that the *Fitzgerald* broke up after sinking: "This placement does not support the theory that the ship plunged to the bottom in one piece, breaking apart when it struck bottom. If this were true, the two sections would be much closer. In addition, the angle, repose and mounding of clay and mud at the site indicate the stern rolled over on the surface, spilling taconite ore pellets from its severed cargo hold, and then landed on portions of the cargo itself."

As controversial as both his expedition and conclusions proved to be, Shannon did make at least one significant discovery during his dives when he came across what was left of the body of a crew member. The man was wearing a life jacket, which suggested two important things. First, the use of a life preserver indicated the crew must have had some sense that the ship was going down. Furthermore, the fact that the man and his life preserver landed at the bottom of the lake indicates that he must have been trapped somewhere inside the ship when it went down, because the buoyancy of the life preserver would have taken him to the surface otherwise. He might still have drowned or suffered hypothermia, but the body would have been found during the initial searches in 1975.

Not long after Shannon finished his dives, Joseph MacInnis led a team that included members of the Harbor Branch Oceanographic Institution and the GLSHS on six dives over the sunken ship as part of the "Great Lakes 94," a six-week expedition exploring the Saint Lawrence River and the Great Lakes. In his report, MacInnis maintained that there was nothing in the information he obtained that could shed further light on the reason for the ship's loss.

In 1995, MacInnis returned to the *Fitzgerald* as part of a project sponsored by the Sault Tribe of Chippewa. Wearing a special diving apparatus called a NEWTSUIT, he went at the request of many of the *Fitzgerald*'s family members, who were still looking for some sort of closure. This time, they had a very specific request: retrieve the ship's bell and bring it to the surface, where it could serve a memorial for those lost. The diving team did retrieve the ship's bell and left a replica bell that differed from the original only in that it was engraved with the names of the 29 men lost. After the bell was returned to the surface, it was turned over to a restoration crew that carefully cleaned and restored it, and it still hangs in the Great Lakes Shipwreck Museum. The bell is rung on November 10 each year to commemorate the deaths of the 29 men who went down on the *Edmund Fitzgerald*.

The bell of the *Edmund Fitzgerald* on display at the Great Lakes Shipwreck Museum

Not surprisingly, the plan to remove the bell met with more than a little controversy. Shannon opposed it, calling the retrieval "the most unethical, self-serving, sneaky approach to artifact removal I have even heard of." Tom Farnquist, who would later oppose return visits to the grave site, disagreed, saying it was "a very clean and delicate, but easy process. We would never undertake such an effort without having a detailed plan to assure the ship wouldn't be harmed."

The second task was one that the crew took on for themselves and was outside the realm of politics and argument. Cheryl Rozman made the comment to one of the divers that her father "enjoyed having a beer; too bad you couldn't bring him one." Using his NEWTSUIT's robotic arms, Bruce Fucco gently placed a beer can carefully in the pilothouse.

Bruce later reported in the National Geographic: "It's cold and dark at 530 feet, but with all the help we're getting from the submersibles, it's like 10 feet. It feels good knowing you're not alone." Others also shared a new sense of camaraderie. Jack Champeau, who lost his brother, admitted, "Since I can't bring Buck's remains home for a proper burial, I'm here to do the next best thing." Bruce Hudson's mother, Ruth, agreed, saying, "Finally, we had our funeral. It's a grave now. There is no reason why anyone should dive to the *Fitzgerald* again. Let them rest in peace."

However, there are still those who disagree with that sentiment. Though the *Fitzgerald* lay untouched by human hands for nearly 20 years, it would be revisited again in September 1995. Terrence Tysall and Mike Zee entered the chilly waters of Lake Superior in order to make contact the lake's most famous grave, and Tysall later described their first contact with the wreckage: "We reached out and grabbed one of those rails. No one's touched that wreck with human hands since it went down…Personally, the most profound impressions I have of the wreck are of extreme darkness, cold and isolation…All of us have suffered loss and it's not an easy thing. The main thing I would love to tell…folks is we did it to pay our respects.' Zee agreed, calling the feeling "awesome" and adding, "It was not an ego trip - it was a challenge." The two also tried to be respectful of where they were and did not touch the ship again, instead swimming around it with bright lights to illuminate the damage.

Perhaps not surprisingly, opinions about that dive were mixed. Cheryl Rozman complained, "Our men are buried there. That's their resting place, and it should be respected as such…It's a sacred place." Tom Farnquist, the executive director of the Great Lakes Shipwreck Historical Society, claimed, "What they did was really in bad taste." On the other hand, Tom Mount, of the International Association of Nitrox & Technical Divers, defended the dive: "There's nothing at all disrespectful about it…one of the most ambitious dives undertaken in the history of wreck diving."

Chapter 7: The Church Bell Chimed

"In a musty old hall in Detroit they prayed, in the 'Maritime Sailors' Cathedral.'

The church bell chimed 'til it rang twenty-nine times for each man on the *Edmund Fitzgerald*.

The legend lives on from the Chippewa on down of the big lake they call 'Gitche Gumee.'

'Superior,' they said, 'never gives up her dead when the gales of November come early!'" – Gordon Lightfoot, "The Wreck of the Edmund Fitzgerald"

It is easy to look at artifacts like bells and plaques and see these as the only memorials left behind for those who died on the *Edmund Fitzgerald*, but such an attitude is shortsighted at best and insensitive at worst, because the captain and crew are still remembered today in the hearts of the family and friends they left behind and the people whose lives their story has touched.

The first memorial was as simple as it was moving. Before daylight on November 11, 1975, the Reverend Richard W. Ingalls drove to his parish at Mariners' Church of Detroit after he had heard of the wreck earlier in the evening during a call from the head of the Dossin Great Lakes Museum. Later Father Ingalls would recall, "Both of us had been in the military and we read between the lines right away. We expected the worst." When it seemed obvious that all hope was lost, Ingalls knew that the people he served would need comforting, so he went to the place where he found the comfort he needed so that he could in turn offer comfort to others.

Slowly climbing the bell tower, he contemplated what he could say to ease the pain the families would be feeling. Fortunately, his first duty was obvious; at the top of the tower's staircase, Ingalls grasped the bell's rope and, with a quiet prayer, began to pull. He rang the bell 29 times that morning, once for each man lost. Then, when the final tone had faded away, he made his way back down to the church's main sanctuary and began to say what he would later call "a personal requiem for the twenty-nine": "With thanksgiving to God for their courage and strength, for the benefits we have received from their labors and for the blessed hope of their everlasting life, we hereby gratefully remember all the mariners of our Great Lakes who have lost their lives." As people began wandering in, alone and in small groups, Ingalls later observed, "That morning there was a sense that everyone was lost."

Ingalls would continue the tradition of tolling the bell 29 times on November 11 of each year for the rest of his life, even after he was made a bishop, and in 2006, as Ingalls lay dying, he sent for his son, Richard Ingalls, Jr. The younger Ingalls had been practicing law while studying for the ministry in his spare time, and at his father's request, the younger Ingalls took his place in the pulpit.

Later in 1975, Canadian singer Gordon Lightfoot wrote and performed "The Wreck of the Edmund Fitzgerald", a song based on the events surrounding the ship's loss. Lightfoot himself later showed up at the memorial marking the 10th anniversary of the ship's loss, and according to Ingalls, Jr., "He didn't want it to be about him, so we took him up a back stairway. We put him in a front pew with his back to the congregation, so they didn't know who he was. We always had a choir member perform the ballad, but when it came time for it, Lightfoot slipped out of his pew, sat on a stool, picked up his acoustic guitar, and played. First, there was a gasp, but after that, you could hear a pin drop." Following the end of the song, Lightfoot asked to address the congregation. He told them, "I made a mistake referring to this as a musty old hall, but I had never been here before. There's nothing musty about this place. It's beautiful. From now on in concert, I'm going to sing rustic old hall instead."

A picture of Gordon Lightfoot (on the far right) in 1965

The second memorial was performed on July 17, 1999 aboard the *USS Mackinaw*, a Coast Guard cutter. Aboard were the friends and family members of many of those lost, and at the designated moment, Father Ingalls stepped in front of the crowd. He was flanked on each side by two wreaths of flowers, both donated by Gordon Lightfoot, and there were also long-stemmed red carnations, one for each of those gone. They were gathered there, he reminded them, to consecrate the waters below their feet as a hallowed ground and final resting place for their loved ones that should never again be disturbed by divers or anyone wanting to explore the wreckage for any political or financial purpose.

After Ingalls finished speaking, others came forward, one by one, including ships' captains, family members, and government officials from both the United States and Canada. Each had had some small or large part to play in making the day possible, and each had something important to share with the others present. Some spoke and others prayed, but all had their say. Ingalls finally offered his own prayer, concluding, "May we all thank God that we are permitted this extraordinary opportunity to have the service of 'Burial at Sea' to bring full flower out Memorial for the Twenty-nine of the stately big Fitz."

A representative then came forward on behalf of each member of the crew, rang the bell brought on board for that purpose, and dropped a red carnation into the water. At the end, one of those responsible for organizing the service came forward to conclude the event with a poem he had chosen for the event:

> "And so, let us remember the love and the strength of the men of the *Edmund Fitzgerald* when we say: 'They are gone.' Gone where? Gone from your sight is all.
>
> "They are just as large in your hearts and prayers as when you last saw them. And just at the moment when you are saying, 'They are gone,' there are old friends and loved ones saying, 'They are here, safe and happy with us!'"

Bibliography

Andra-Warner, Elle (2006). *Edmund Fitzgerald: The Legendary Great Lakes Shipwreck*. Grand Marais, Minnesota: North Shore Press.

Edwards, Jack (2000). *Big Fitz*. Chicago, Illinois: Wayne Rigby Literacy.

Hemming, Robert J. (1981). *The Gales of November: The Sinking of the* Edmund Fitzgerald. Charlotte, North Carolina: Baker and Taylor, Inc. for Thunder Bay Press.

Kantar, Andrew (1998). *29 Missing: The True and Tragic Story of the Disappearance of the SS* Edmund Fitzgerald. East Lansing, Michigan: Michigan State University Press.

MacInnis, Joseph (1998). Fitzgerald's *Storm: The Wreck of the* Edmund Fitzgerald. Charlotte, North Carolina: Baker and Taylor, Inc. for Thunder Bay Press.

Ramsey, Raymond. (2009). *SS* Edmund Fitzgerald: *Requiem for the Toledo Express*. Houghton, Michigan: Keweenaw Productions..

Schumacher, Michael (2005). *Mighty* Fitz: *The Sinking of the* Edmund Fitzgerald. New York and London: Bloomsbury Publishing.

Stonehouse, Frederick (2006) [1977]. *The Wreck of the* Edmund Fitzgerald (6th ed.). Gwinn,

Michigan: Avery Color Studios.

―― (1994). *Queen of the Lakes*. Detroit, Michigan: Wayne State University Press.

CPSIA information can be obtained
at www.ICGtesting.com
Printed in the USA
LVHW080548290822
727064LV00008B/429

9 781500 234775